DON'T SE
Receiving Go

RECEIVING
GOD'S
ABUNDANT
BEST

DON'T
SETTLE
FOR LESS

DEREK PRINCE

DON'T SETTLE FOR LESS
Receiving God's Abundant Best

© 1985 by Derek Prince Ministries-International
This edition published by Derek Prince Ministries-UK 2019
Previously published under the title: If You Want God's Best

ISBN   978-1-78263-669-4
ePub   978-1-78263-670-0
Kindle   978-1-78263-671-7
Product Code T110 EN3

Derek Prince Ministries · www.derekprince.com
Set in Arno by Raphael Freeman, Renana Typesetting

The title of this book is a challenge:
Don't settle for less!
The introductory word 'don't'
immediately confronts you with a choice.
Do you want God's best … or don't you?
Your answer to this question leaves room for me
to share with you eight things you will need to do
if you decide that you really don't want to settle
for less then receiving God's abundant best.

– Derek Prince

CONTENTS

A Fertile Heart

Our personal relationship with God is never one-sided or a one-way street. There are always two sides; there are always two directions. On the one hand, there is what God makes available to us; on the other hand, there is how we respond to what God makes available. The kind of life we actually experience will be determined by the interplay of what God makes available to us and how we respond to it.

This is very clearly illustrated by the Parable of the Sower. This parable is about a man who went out to sow seed in a field and the seed fell on four different kinds of soil. First, some seed fell beside the beaten path and, because the ground was hard and beaten down by the feet of those that passed by, the seed never even entered the soil. As a result, the birds of the air ate the seed and it produced nothing.

Second, some of the seed fell onto rocky ground. The seed went down a little way where its roots met rock and it started to grow up too quickly with no depth of root. So when the sun became hot it withered and it, too, produced nothing.

The third kind of soil was called "among thorns," where the thorns grew up together with the seed and eventually choked it. It did not get enough air and nourishment and so it, too, brought forth nothing permanent of good.

Finally, the fourth kind of soil is what is described as "good ground."

I do not want to deal with the first three kinds of soil. I want to focus on what I regard as the climax of that parable; the objective to which Jesus is working, which is the *good ground*. I trust that I am addressing people whose heart is good ground. This is what Jesus said about the good ground and the seed that fell on it:

*But what was sown on good soil is the man who
hears the word and understands it. He produces
a crop, yielding a hundred, sixty or thirty times
what was sown.*   Matthew 13:23

Notice there are two key factors in the man
who produces a crop: first, he hears the word and,
second, he understands it. This is true of every-
body who represents good soil. However, even
though all the people who represent good soil
bring forth a crop, there is a very important difference in the level of yield they produce: some
produce a hundred times, some sixty and some
only thirty times what was sown. In other words,
for each seed sown, some produce a hundred
seeds, some produce sixty seeds and some produce thirty seeds. It is interesting to observe that
the hundredfold yield is more than the sum of
the other sixty and thirtyfold yields put together.
This principle runs through the Word of God.
The people who really make it through to full
productiveness are much more productive than
the people who are only partly productive.

I want to focus on *the hundredfold* which

is representative of the people who want and achieve God's best. In another version of the same parable found in Luke 8:15, Jesus makes particular reference to the good soil:

> *"But the seed on good soil stands for those with a noble and good heart, who hear the word, retain it, and by persevering produce a crop."*

In that description there are two vitally important factors which are both related to our theme of wanting God's best. First, there is the kind of heart. It is described as noble and good. An alternative translation for "noble" is "honest." So, the first requirement is honesty, openness or sincerity. This means not covering anything up or having double standards. That is the first requirement.

Second, there is a threefold response from these people: they *hear* the word, they *retain* it and, by *persevering*, they produce a crop. Those three factors are extremely important and I want to emphasize them in connection with our theme. Above all, *persevering* is a key to this theme of wanting God's best.

The principle unfolded in this parable confronts each of us with a personal decision. I cannot overemphasize the importance of decision in the walk of faith. So many people do not realize that the course of our lives depends ultimately upon the decisions we make and *not* on our feelings.

The decision that confronts each one of us is: how much do I intend to produce? Will I be satisfied with thirty times? Do I intend to produce sixty times? Or am I aiming for God's best and intend to produce one hundred times? You are confronted with the necessity of making this decision. The very fact that you are reading this teaching automatically confronts you with a decision: do I want God's best? Am I going to aim at a hundredfold or be content with sixty- or thirtyfold?

What you achieve will depend on the response of your heart. I pointed out earlier that there are two sides to our relationship with God. One side is what God makes available to us, the other side is how we respond to what God makes available. What will be decisive in your life is *how you respond.*

In the parable we quoted from the interpretation in Luke 8, we saw there were three aspects to the successful response: first, hearing God's Word; second, retaining it; and third, persevering in what you are doing.

In the sections that follow, I will explain certain things that are necessary if you want God's best. I will give you certain specific applications of these principles. This will be based on three things: first, on Scripture; second, on my own personal experience, which extends well over forty years; and third, on my observation of others. I have had the privilege of being associated with many Christians from different backgrounds, races and countries, and I have tried to particularly observe those whom I consider to be successful, "hundredfold" people. I have tried to learn from their lives the principles of success. That is what I will be sharing with you – the principles of success, what you will have to do if you want God's best.

CHAPTER 2

God Has Made Full Provision

I want to share two important scriptural facts related to being productive or to bearing fruit. I believe that if you can understand these two facts, they will create in you the faith that you need to be fully productive. The first fact is this: God *wants us all to be fruitful.* This is a settled matter of the will of God. It is not something that is going to change. It is true right from God's creation of man. It was the very purpose for which God created man. This is stated in Genesis 1:27–28, where we read an account of God's creation of man and of the purpose for which He created him.

So God created man in his own image, in the image of God he created him; male and female he created them. God blessed them and said to them, "Be fruitful and increase in number; fill the earth and subdue it. Rule over the fish of the sea and the birds of the air and over every living creature that moves on the ground."

There are five things God wanted man to do:

1. Be fruitful
2. Increase
3. Fill
4. Subdue
5. Rule

That is the purpose for which man was created. God's purposes never change. Their fulfillment may be delayed by man's failure but, ultimately, God is always going to go ahead and achieve His purpose.

In the new creation, in Jesus Christ, the same purposes of God are restored once again. This is made very clear in many places in the New Testament. In particular there is a prayer of the apostle Paul for the Christians with whom he was dealing. This beautiful prayer is recorded in Colossians 1:9–12 and has a totally positive emphasis. Every word in this prayer is positive; there is not one negative word in the whole of this prayer.

> *For this reason, since the day we heard about you, we have not stopped praying for you and asking God to fill you with the knowledge of his will through all spiritual wisdom and understanding. And we pray this in order that you may live a life worthy of the Lord and may please him in every way: bearing fruit in every good work, growing in the knowledge of God, being strengthened with all power according to his glorious might so that you may have great endurance and patience, and joyfully giving thanks to the Father, who has qualified you to share in the inheritance of the saints in the kingdom of light.*

Let me point out all the positive words. First, Paul speaks about us being *filled with the knowledge* of God's will – not just having somewhere in us the knowledge of God's will, but being *filled* with it. This comes *through all spiritual wisdom and understanding* – not just some, but *all* spiritual wisdom. Then he prays that they may *live a life pleasing to the Lord in every way* – not just pleasing Him in some ways, but pleasing Him in *every* way. He prays that they may bear fruit in *every good work* – that is the hundredfold growing in the knowledge of God. Then, *being strengthened with all power according to His glorious might* – not some power, but *all* power – with the result that we may have great endurance.

Perseverance or *endurance* was one of the key words in the Parable of the Sower. Here Paul wants us to have great *endurance* and *patience* and *joy*. Finally, Paul uses the statement that God the Father *has qualified* [us] *to share in the inheritance of the saints in the kingdom of light*. God has given us the provision that is needed to enter into our inheritance in the kingdom of light.

God's will is settled forever in the Word of God. He wants us to be fruitful, He wants us to bear fruit, to succeed in every good work and to please Him in every way. He has also qualified us or equipped us to do this.

We have seen already that God wants us to be fruitful in every good work. This is the will of

God. There is no question about His will – the question is our response to His will.

The second fact that I want to emphasize is: *God has made full provision for this.* We have seen from Paul's prayer that God has equipped us or qualified us to take our place in the "inheritance of the saints in the kingdom of light." This truth is brought out in many ways in the New Testament. Here is a very powerful statement that God has made full provision for this.

> *His divine power has given us everything we need for life and godliness through our knowledge of him who called us by his own glory and goodness. Through these he has given us his very great and precious promises, so that through them you may participate in the divine nature and escape the corruption in the world caused by evil desires.* 2 Peter 1:3–4

Notice that opening phrase, "[God's] divine power." His total omnipotence, His unlimited power, "... has given us *everything* we need." Let me emphasize that God has given us everything we need for life and godliness. This is provided in two related ways: first, "...through the knowledge of Him who has called us"; that is, through the knowledge of Jesus Christ. Then, second, "...through his very great and precious promises." The provision comes through knowing Jesus Christ and through appropriating the promises of God's Word. There is a phrase I use in this connection which I think I can never say too often: *The provision is in the promises.* In the promises of God's Word is contained all the provision we are ever going to need. You might say, "Well, if God has given us full provision, where is it?" The answer is: it is all in the promises of God's Word. As you appropriate those promises, you discover the provision.

There are two marvelous results of appropriating the promises. The first is that we participate in the divine nature. The very nature of God Himself comes into us and we begin to share in His own divine nature. Second, the logical negative consequence is that we escape the corruption that is in the world caused by evil desires. How do you feel about the possibility of becoming partaker of God's own nature and escaping the corruption that is in this world through evil desires? Doesn't that appeal to you? God has made full provision for that. He has made it possible for you and me to do that. Everything we need has already been given us.

Thus, we have two sides. On your side, *if* you want God's best; and on God's side, He *does* want it for you and has made full provision for you. So, the key decision is: do you want God's best? That is one thing God will not do for you. He will not make the decision for you. You must make the decision for yourself.

CHAPTER 3

Settle for Nothing Less

In this theme, "If You Want God's Best," the number one requirement is *want God's best*. Can you see that? If you want God's best, the first thing you have to do is make up your mind that you do *want* God's best. This is the basic key decision. You have to want God's best and you have to decide that you will settle for nothing less than God's best. God will not force this choice on us. It rests with us to make this decision.

I want to illustrate this principle from the story of the twin brothers, Jacob and Esau. I want to bring out of their story what I consider to be the key principle. There are some very remarkable statements made by God in

Scripture about Jacob and Esau. For example, in Malachi 1:2–3 the Lord speaks to Israel, who are the descendants of Jacob, and says this:

"Was not Esau Jacob's brother?" [The answer is: Yes, indeed, his twin brother.] *"Yet I have loved Jacob, but Esau I have hated."*

Notice that. They were twin brothers but God says He loved Jacob and hated Esau. God's attitude toward the two brothers was totally opposite. He loved one of them and hated the other. This is commented on still further by the apostle Paul in Romans 9:10–13, where he says this concerning these twin brothers:

Not only that, but Rebecca's children had one and the same father, our father Isaac. Yet, before the twins were born or had done anything good or bad – in order that God's purpose in election might stand: not by works but by him who calls – she [Rebecca] *was told, "The older* [Esau] *will serve the younger* [Jacob]." *Just as it is written: "Jacob I loved, but Esau I hated."*

Not only were Jacob and Esau born of the same mother, they were born of the same father – they were absolute twins. But Jacob was preferred over Esau before they were even born, even though they were twins.

This passage from Romans raises two very important questions. First: what did God see in Jacob that He approved? Second: what did God see in Esau that He disapproved? In short, why did God love Jacob but hate Esau?

Let me briefly sketch their characters for you, as unfolded in Scripture, starting with Esau. Esau was a "good guy," "a nice chap." He was strong, active, manly, a hunter. He did no one any harm. He was the favorite of his father. And he was no match for his shrewd twin brother, Jacob, who outdid him every time they had a confrontation.

What about Jacob? He was shrewd, determined, unscrupulous. He never got the worst of a bargain. That is a quality which nobody really likes. He obtained the birthright from Esau for a bowl of soup. When his brother was hungry, he persuaded him to sell that priceless birthright for nothing more than a bowl of soup. If ever there was a bargain, that was it! He deceived his father to obtain the blessing, and he gained a fortune at the expense of Laban, who was both his uncle and his father-in-law. By no means would anyone consider Jacob a "nice guy" or a "good chap." By contemporary standards, most people would prefer Esau. But God did not.

Why did God prefer Jacob? I am going to offer you one basic reason, which I believe is the key to it all. *Jacob appreciated what God had to give; Esau was indifferent.*

In Hebrews 12:15–17 we get a scriptural estimate of what God thinks of indifference. His views of indifference are very different than those of most Christians. Commenting on Esau's behavior, the writer of Hebrews says:

> *See to it that no one misses the grace of God and that no bitter root grows up to cause trouble and defile many. See that no one is sexually immoral, or is godless like Esau, who for a single meal sold his inheritance rights as the oldest son. Afterward, as you know, when he wanted to inherit this blessing, he was rejected. He could bring about no change of mind, though he sought the blessing with tears.*

Notice how Esau is described. He is described as "godless" and he is put on the same level with the sexually immoral. He is also described as "godless" because for a single meal, a bowl of soup, he sold his inheritance rights. About this Scripture says, "Esau despised his birthright." You must understand that by God's standards to be indifferent concerning what God has to offer is "godless" and God hates it.

Let's look at the opposite side: Jacob's attitude toward what God had to offer. I will take just one key incident. Jacob was on his way back to his own land when he met a man at night who was also an angel or a messenger from God. As you will remember, he wrestled with this man all night. This is so typical of Jacob because he was a wrestler.

> So Jacob was left alone, and a man wrestled with him till daybreak. When the man saw that he could not overpower him, he touched the socket of Jacob's hip so that his hip was wrenched as he wrestled with the man. Then the man said, "Let me go, for it is daybreak." But Jacob replied,

"I will not let you go unless you bless me." The man asked him, "What is your name?" "Jacob," he answered. Then the man said, "Your name will no longer be Jacob, but Israel, because you have struggled with God and with men and have overcome." Genesis 32:24–28

The meaning of Israel, as there interpreted, is "struggling with God." How typical! Jacob was a struggler, a wrestler – but he had one key principle, he wanted God's best. He said to this angel, "I will not let you go unless you bless me." I believe that was the key to God's favor toward Jacob. God did not condone the flaws in Jacob's character; God never does. But because Jacob would not settle for less than God's best, God was gradually able to deal with him and to make out of him the kind of man He wanted him to be. The condition was the starting point that Jacob would not settle for anything less than God's best.

I want to ask you: will you make the same decision, that you will not settle for anything less than God's best?

CHAPTER 4

Focus on Jesus

There is a second way to complete the sentence: "If you want God's best." It is *focus on Jesus*.

> *Therefore, since we are surrounded by such a great cloud of witnesses, let us throw off everything that hinders and the sin that so easily entangles, and let us run with perseverance the race marked out for us. Let us fix our eyes on Jesus, the author and perfecter of our faith....*
>
> Hebrews 12:1–2

There are a number of logical steps in what the writer says. First, he points out that we are surrounded by a great cloud of witnesses. He is referring to the previous chapter of Hebrews (chapter 11), where he spoke about the great saints of the Old Testament who succeeded, men who found God's best. The writer says we have a cloud of witnesses around us, people who have proved in their life and experience that it really is possible to find God's best. That is the starting point.

Second, he says that if we want to find God's best, it will consist in running a race. In order to run the race successfully we must throw off everything that hinders. A runner does not carry a single ounce of unnecessary weight on his person or in his clothing. In our case, it is the sin that so easily entangles us, and we must be sure there is nothing to trip us up.

Third, we must run with perseverance. I pointed out earlier, in connection with the good soil in the Parable of the Sower, that the three conditions were hearing the Word, retaining the Word and bringing forth fruit with perseverance.

Having laid those foundations for success, the writer of Hebrews now comes to what I consider to be the critical point. "Let us fix our eyes

on Jesus, the author and perfecter of our faith. "
This is a key to success: focus on Jesus, keep your
eyes on Him. The writer points out that Jesus
is both the *author* and *perfecter* of our faith.

To use two other simpler words, He is the
beginner of our faith and the *completer* of our faith.
We probably all realize that Jesus is the beginner,
but sometimes we forget the fact that Jesus is
also the completer. If we want our faith to be
completed, we have to go on focusing on Jesus.
It is not enough to begin by focusing on Jesus
and then get distracted and look away somewhere else. If we do that, our faith will never be
completed.

In this connection, I want to point out to you
three simple facts, each of which is a reason why
we should continue to focus on Jesus.

1. JESUS IS OUR LORD. We can only enter into
   salvation through confessing Jesus as our
   Lord. If He is our Lord, then our supreme
   purpose is to please Him. That is what it
   means when we say that He is our Lord. We
   need to continually keep our eyes on Jesus
   to make sure that everything we are doing

pleases Him. If at any time as we look at Him we get an indication that what we are considering would not please Him, that is a sufficient reason for not doing it. But we cannot receive such an indication unless we keep our eyes fixed on Jesus.

2. JESUS IS THE ONLY STANDARD OF RIGHTEOUSNESS. This is brought out by a statement that Paul made to the men of Athens.

[God] *has appointed a day on which He will judge the world in righteousness by the Man whom He has ordained. He has given assurance of this to all, by raising Him from the dead.*

Acts 17:31

The One who is going to be God's judge of the world is the man whom He raised from the dead, Jesus Christ. God is going to judge the world in righteousness by that Man.

That tells us two things: Jesus is the judge, and He is also the standard of righteousness. We are going to be judged by the standard of Jesus. It is important to see that God has only one standard of righteousness. If we want to know what is righteous in the eyes of God, the ultimate place we must look for the answer is always Jesus. We may look at Christians who do the things that Jesus would not have done, but we cannot accept them as our standard of righteousness because that is not God's standard. To find out God's standard of righteousness we must keep our eyes focused on Jesus.

3. JESUS IS OUR PATTERN OR OUR EXAMPLE.

To this you were called, because Christ suffered for you, leaving you an example, that you should follow in his steps. 1 Peter 2:21

Jesus is our example because He has gone the way ahead of us. To follow in the right path we must see where He planted His steps and plant our footsteps in the same places. All of that is involved in this one important requirement: that we focus on Jesus by keeping our eyes fixed on Him.

I want to give you one more important reason why it is necessary to focus on Jesus. It is a very simple reason, a very practical reason, but a very important one. The whole gospel centers in what Jesus has done for us. This is stated so clearly by Paul in first Corinthians. Notice there are orders of importance in the things of God, but these things that Paul now speaks of are of first importance. He makes three simple statements, each of which relates to Jesus:

> *For what I received I passed on to you as of first importance: that Christ died for our sins according to the Scriptures, that he was buried, that he was raised on the third day according to the Scriptures.* 1 Corinthians 15:3–4

That is the gospel. Those are the facts of the first importance. Everything else is of secondary importance in the gospel compared with those three facts, all of which center in Jesus: that He died; that He was buried; that He arose again the third day. We can never afford to let anything else become more important than those three facts about Jesus. We must be careful never to be enticed away from these basic truths centered in Jesus.

Paul warns Timothy of this in his second epistle to Timothy written from prison very near the end of his life.

Remember Jesus Christ, raised from the dead, descended from David. This is my gospel, for which I am suffering even to the point of being chained like a criminal. But God's word is not chained. 2 Timothy 2:8–9

Notice those key words, "Remember Jesus Christ, raised from the dead . . . This is my gospel." How simple! It is just like what he says in 1 Corinthians 15, the whole gospel message centers in Jesus: His death, His burial and His victorious resurrection.

He also tells Timothy to never get distracted from these central points, but to keep his eyes focused on Jesus.

There is a great danger for Christians to become too sophisticated or too spiritual. Many Christians lose out by becoming too spiritual. People sometimes say to me after I preach, "Brother Prince, that was a deep message." And I find myself wondering, "Did I do something wrong?" In a certain sense, I do not want to go too deep. I never want to go so deep that people lose sight of Jesus and the central facts of the gospel: His death, His burial, His resurrection.

Let me exhort you with what Paul said to Timothy: "Remember Jesus Christ, raised from the dead." One very important practical way to remember Jesus is through the taking of communion or the Lord's Supper. Jesus said, "Do this, as often as you do it, in remembrance of Me." It is a very simple, scriptural, practical way to remember Jesus and to keep your eyes focused on Him. Remember, He said, "Do it as *often* as you do it," not as seldom as you do it.

CHAPTER 5

Meditate in God's Word

A third thing that it is most important for you to do if you want God's best is: *meditate in God's Word*. Fill your mind with the Word of God. Let us look at the example of Joshua and the instructions the Lord gave him as he was about to lead Israel into their inheritance.

> *"This Book of the Law shall not depart from your mouth, but you shall meditate in it day and night, that you may observe to do according to all that is written in it. For then you will make your way prosperous, and then you will have good success."*   Joshua 1:8

That last phrase, "…you will make your way prosperous, and then you will have good success," is equivalent to saying, "…you will find God's best." What are the conditions? They are threefold and they all relate to God's Word.

- First, the Word is *not to depart from your mouth*.
- Second, you are *to meditate in it day and night* – that means continually.
- Third, you are *to observe to do according to all that is written in it.*

I have sometimes summed it up in three simple phrases. If you want God's best and want to make your way prosperous and have good success, these are the three things you must do: think God's Word, speak God's Word, and act God's Word. I put thinking first because if you do not think, you will never fully speak. If you do not think and speak, you will never fully act. The result totals success – God's best.

You might say, "That was Joshua. How do I know that will work for me?" The first psalm has a similar promise with a similar instruction, and it is for anybody who meets the conditions. It is all-inclusive. It does not matter who the person is, all that matters is that the person meets the conditions.

Blessed is the man who does not walk in the counsel of the wicked or stand in the way of sinners or sit in the seat of mockers. But his delight is in the law of the Lord, and on his law he meditates day and night. He is like a tree planted by streams of water, which yields its fruit in season and whose leaf does not wither. Whatever he does prospers. Psalm 1:1–3

Notice the closing sentence: "Whatever he does prospers." That is finding God's best; that is true success. This can be true of any man who meets the conditions. The conditions are five-fold. The first three are negative things you must *not* do:

1. You must not walk in the counsel of the wicked
2. You must not stand in the way of sinners
3. You must not sit in the seat of mockers

The key issue is where you get your counsel from. If you get your counsel from the wrong source, then your whole life will go wrong. It is then followed by the two positive conditions:

4. His delight is in the law of the Lord
5. On his law he meditates day and night

Notice that both of the positive conditions center around the law of the Lord or the Word of God. First, you have to delight yourself in His law. Second, you have to meditate on it day and night. Notice again that right meditation is the key to success – meditating in God's Word day and night.

That does not mean just spending ten minutes a day reading your Bible, but it means to so fill your mind with the Bible that it occupies your thoughts all the day long. You are always feeding on that which is positive, faith-inspiring and upbuilding. What you think really will be decisive in how you live. I have sometimes said that human personality is like an iceberg, seven-eighths is below the surface. Very little of the iceberg actually shows above the surface in comparison with what is below the surface. It is also true with human personality. What the person is thinking about is going to determine the course of his or her life. If you meditate on the right thing and live the right kind of life then you get the results that God has promised: success and prosperity – God's best.

Let us look at a passage from the prophet Isaiah which reiterates that the way we think is decisive to our experience. God is speaking in Isaiah 55:8–13:

> *"For my thoughts are not your thoughts,*
>> *neither are your ways my ways"*
>> *declares the Lord.*
>> *"As the heavens are higher than the earth,*
>> *so are my ways higher*
>> *than your ways and my thoughts than*
>> *your thoughts.*
>> *As the rain and the snow come down from*
>> *heaven, and do not return to it*
>> *without watering the earth*
>> *and making it bud and flourish,*
>> *so that it yields seed for the sower*
>> *and bread for the eater,*
>> *so is my word that goes out from my*
>>> *mouth."*

Notice God begins with thoughts and He says by nature our thoughts are not God's thoughts. How then can we begin to think God's thoughts? God gives the answer in the words that follow. God's ways and God's thoughts are on the heavenly plane and our ways and our thoughts are on the earthly plane, far below God's. But God's Word brings His ways and His thoughts down from heaven into our lives and hearts, which produces the results we need.

God goes on to say in Isaiah 55:11, concerning His Word:

> *"It will not return to me empty,*
> *but will accomplish what I desire*
> *and achieve the purpose for which I sent it.*
> *You will go out in joy*
> *and be led forth in peace;*
> *the mountains and hills*
> *will burst into song before you,*
> *and all the trees of the field*
> *will clap their hands.*
> *Instead of the thornbush will grow the pine*
> *tree, and instead of briers the myrtle will*
> *grow."*

This is the result of God's Word coming down from heaven, entering our hearts, occupying our minds and replacing our ways and our thoughts with God's ways and God's thoughts. God's Word brings His ways and thoughts down to our hearts and lives. As our minds are filled with the Word of God, we begin to think the thoughts of God. Our whole thought-life is completely changed.

The results are stated here in beautiful language: *peace*, you shall go out with peace; *joy*, you will go out with joy; *praise*, even the things of nature will praise, "the trees of the field will clap their hands"; and *fruitfulness*, in place of the thornbush and the brier, the myrtle and the pine will grow. That is what happens in our lives when God's Word comes in and we receive it and begin to meditate on it. Our own ways and our own thoughts are like the thorns and the briers, they are unproductive and unhelpful. But when they are replaced by God's Word, then instead of the thorn and the brier we bring forth the pine and the myrtle.

I want to suggest that you should view the substitution of God's ways and God's thoughts for your own ways and thoughts as being the key to success. You should also cultivate the practice of meditating in God's Word day and night. Meditating in God's Word is learning to think God's thoughts after Him through His Word received into our hearts and minds.

CHAPTER 6

Make Friends With the Holy Spirit

The fourth thing you must do "If you want God's best," is *make friends with the Holy Spirit*. I deliberately use a phrase that suggests the personality of the Holy Spirit. For many Christians, the Holy Spirit is a kind of theological abstraction. They accept that God the Father is a person, they accept that Jesus Christ is a person, but they have no concept that the Holy Spirit is a person. Yet, scripturally and theologically, this is a fact. The Holy Spirit is a person just as much as the Father and the Son.

He is also compared to a dove. One of the

important features of a dove is that it is a timid creature and if you do not respond in the right way to the presence of a dove it will just fly off. I think that is true of the Holy Spirit. In a certain sense, He is timid. If we do not respond to Him the right way, He just takes off.

I would like to quote a passage of Scripture where Jesus speaks to His disciples about the Holy Spirit as a person and what the Holy Spirit should do in our lives.

> *"I have much more to say to you, more than you can now bear. But when he, the Spirit of truth, comes, he will guide you into all truth. He will not speak on his own; he will speak only what he hears, and he will tell you what is yet to come. He will bring glory to me by taking from what is mine and making it known to you. All that belongs to the Father is mine. That is why I said the Spirit will take from what is mine and make it known to you."* John 16:12–15

First, Jesus does everything that language permits to emphasize the personality of the Holy Spirit by saying, "But when he, the Spirit of truth, comes...." In the Greek language in which these words are given to us, there are three genders: masculine, feminine, and neuter. Neuter is the "it" gender. In Greek, the word for "spirit," *pneuma*, is neuter. In other words, the normal pronoun to use with "spirit" would be "it." But Jesus breaks the law of grammar and says not "when it," but "when he, the Spirit of truth, comes." In other words, He goes out of His way to emphasize that we are dealing with a person.

Jesus then speaks about various things the Holy Spirit will do. He will report on what He hears from heaven by bringing us the latest news from heaven; He will show us what is yet to come by unfolding the future to us.

Then Jesus says, "...he will bring glory to me by taking from what is mine and making it known to you. All that belongs to the Father is mine." That is extremely important. Everything the Father has belongs to the Son, and everything the Son has, the Spirit administers. If you put that together, the Holy Spirit is the administrator of the total wealth of the Godhead. All that the Father has and all that the Son has, they have in common. But it is the Holy Spirit who takes from the wealth of the Father and the Son and makes it available to us. Thus, you can be a child of God legally and doctrinally, and yet live a very poor and inadequate kind of life unless you relate rightly to the Holy Spirit because the Holy Spirit is the administrator of the total wealth of the Godhead.

Again, in John 14:15–18 Jesus says to His disciples:

> *"If you love me, you will obey what I command. And I will ask the Father, and he will give you another Counselor to be with you forever – the Spirit of truth. The world cannot accept him, because it neither sees him nor knows him. But you know him, for he lives with you and will be in you. I will not leave you as orphans, I will come to you."*

Notice two vitally important facts: first, Jesus comes to us in the Holy Spirit; second, unless we relate rightly to the Holy Spirit, we are like orphans even though we are truly sons of God. You see, it is the Holy Spirit alone who enables us to live as true sons of God. This is brought out very clearly by Paul in Romans 8:14:

For as many as are led by the Spirit of God [and that's a continuing present tense – as many as are being continually led by the Spirit of God], *these are sons of God.*

The word that is used for "sons" here implies maturity; not merely babies or infants, but grown sons of God. We are babies when we become born again by the Holy Spirit. But, in order to become mature sons of God, we need a further, ongoing relationship to the Holy Spirit. We must be continually led by the Holy Spirit and Paul says that it is very definitive, " … as many as are [being continually] led by the Spirit of God, these are the sons of God." Thus, to become a child of God you have to be born again of the Holy Spirit; but, to become a mature son of God, you must have an ongoing relationship by being daily and continually led by the Holy Spirit.

I observe in the Church today that there are many who are truly born of God but who are not regularly led by God. They know the new birth, but they do not know that continuing relationship to the Holy Spirit which alone can enable them to live as mature sons of God. So, if you want God's best, you must cultivate an ongoing relationship with the Holy Spirit as a person. He is your personal guide, the administrator of the riches of the kingdom of God, who alone can impart all these things to you in experience.

There is one further important fact in our relationship to the Holy Spirit. We must be respectful and sensitive toward the Holy Spirit. Paul brings this out clearly in Ephesians 4:30–31.

And do not grieve the Holy Spirit of God, with whom you were sealed for the day of redemption. Get rid of all bitterness, rage and anger, brawling and slander, along with every form of malice.

You remember that we said at the beginning, the Holy Spirit is compared to a dove, a timid bird that is easily scared away. So, when Paul says, "…do not grieve the Holy Spirit," he means, "Don't scare that dove away." He then mentions the things that scare the dove: bitterness, rage, anger, brawling, slander, along with every form of malice. We must be very sensitive in not saying or doing anything that would frighten away that beautiful, sensitive dove because He is the only one that can bring us into our inheritance and enable us to live daily as mature sons of God.

CHAPTER 7

Hear and Obey God's Word

We now come to a fifth way to complete the sentence: "If you want God's best." You must *learn to hear and obey God's voice.*

This is not something that comes to us naturally. In a certain sense, the old Adamic nature is born deaf to the voice of God. It is not natural for the old carnal nature to hear God's voice. It is something that must be learned and cultivated with care. The world today is full of innumerable voices that blast us, that crowd in upon us, that demand our attention. Yet, in the midst of it all, there is that still, small voice of God which has endless wisdom and authority, and which is the key to our well-being.

I want to suggest to you that there is tremendous motivation revealed in Scripture for cultivating the ability to hear the voice of God. The success of our relationship to God and our walk with Him depends on hearing His voice.

I would like to give a few specific examples. First, in the matter of receiving healing and health from God. Without question, the Scripture makes it clear that the key to healing and health is the ability to hear God's voice. This is brought out so clearly in Exodus 15:26, where Moses is speaking to the children of Israel:

"If you diligently heed the voice of the Lord your God and do what is right in His sight, give ear to His commandments and keep all His statutes, I will put none of the diseases on you which I have brought on the Egyptians. For I am the Lord who heals you."

The Hebrew says, "If hearing, you hear the voice of the Lord your God." That is a Hebraism, a very emphatic form. It means to listen with the most tremendous care to the voice of the Lord

44

your God. Then God offers to be your personal physician. But the basic condition is to diligently listen to the voice of the Lord.

In Deuteronomy 28:1–2 Moses reveals that the key to all God's blessings is hearing and obeying His voice.

> *"Now it shall come to pass, if you diligently obey the voice of the Lord your God to observe carefully all His commandments which I command you today, that the Lord your God will set you on high above all nations of the earth. All these blessings shall come upon you and overtake you, because you obey the voice of the Lord your God."*

Notice, twice Moses says that the key condition is hearing and obeying the voice of God. He says if you do that "all these blessings will come upon you and overtake you." You do not need to pursue the blessings, they will pursue you if you cultivate hearing the voice of God. On the other hand, a little farther on in verse 15, he warns that if we fail to hear the voice of the Lord our God, it will be the exact opposite: instead of blessings it will be curses.

> *"But it shall come to pass, if you do not obey the voice of the Lord your God, to observe carefully all His commandments and His statutes which I command you today, that all these curses will come upon you and overtake you."*
>
> Deuteronomy 28:15

So, failure to hear and obey the voice of the Lord brings upon us all the curses; hearing and obeying brings all the blessings. That is the watershed between blessing and cursing. It is either hearing and obeying the voice of the Lord or failing to hear and obey the voice of the Lord.

In Jeremiah 7:22–23, the Lord lays this down as the key condition for being His people. He says to Israel:

> *"I did not speak to your fathers, or command them in the day that I brought them out of the land of Egypt, concerning burnt offerings or sacrifices. But this is what I commanded them, saying, 'Obey My voice, and I will be your God, and you shall be My people.'"*

God is saying here that the ordinances of the law relating to the temple, the priesthood and the sacrifices are secondary. The first thing He required of them when He brought them out of Egypt was not sacrifice, offering or a lot of legal requirements. He required them to hear and obey His voice. By implication, He is saying that the sacrifices are good if they proceed out of hearing His voice, but if they were to merely offer sacrifices without hearing His voice, it would not qualify them to be His people. They would be His people only if they would hear and obey the voice of God.

That is the most concise statement in Scripture about what it is to be God's people: "Obey My voice, and I will be your God, and you shall be My people."

This does not change in the New Testament, where the condition for belonging to Jesus Christ is just the same. Jesus states it very simply in John 10:27: "My sheep hear my voice, and I know them, and they follow Me."

Who are "my sheep"? They are the people of Jesus. They are not necessarily Catholics, Protestants, Baptists, Methodists or any other particular denomination. The people that belong to Jesus are the people who hear His voice and follow Him. If you do not hear His voice, you cannot follow Him. That is always the mark of God's true people: *hearing His voice.*

I want to give you two important warnings in connection with this theme of hearing God's voice. First, *cultivate prompt obedience,* and I want to emphasize *prompt.* Abraham is set forth in the Bible as an example for all who believe, and one of the ways in which he is an example is that whenever he heard God's voice, he obeyed Him promptly, without delay. Here is an example in Genesis 22:2–3:

> *Then He* [the Lord] *said, "Take now your son, your only son Isaac, whom you love, and go to the land of Moriah, and offer him there as a burnt offering on one of the mountains of which I shall tell you." So Abraham rose early in the morning and saddled his donkey, and took two of his young men with him, and Isaac his son."*

Notice, Abraham rose early in the morning the next day. As soon as it was possible he set out to obey what he had heard God say to him. I can tell you from experience and from observation that the longer you delay to obey God, the harder it becomes. The only easy way to obey God is to obey Him promptly, the first time He speaks.

Let us look at a negative example: somebody who delayed in obeying God was Lot's wife. She was willing to come out of Sodom but she came so slowly she never made it. She looked back and was turned into a pillar of salt. One of the shortest verses in the New Testament in the teaching of Jesus is in Luke 17:32: "Remember Lot's wife." In other words, do not delay to obey, it may be too late.

The second warning I want to give you is to *be prepared to seem foolish in the eyes of people.* In 1 Corinthians 1:25 Paul says, "the foolishness of God is wiser than men and the weakness of God is stronger than men." If you believe that what people think is wise, you may miss God. In 1 Corinthians 3:18 Paul is very emphatic:

Let no one deceive himself. If anyone among you seems to be wise in this age, let him become a fool that he may become wise.

To become truly wise, you have to start by becoming a fool. Many people stumble on that, but there are many examples in the Bible. Noah built a ship on dry land when no one had ever seen rain. That was foolish, but it was the wisdom of God. Naaman, the captain of Syria, went down into the River Jordan and exposed his leprous flesh by dipping himself seven times. How foolish! But he was healed. Then there was the man born blind in John chapter 9. Jesus placed clay on his eyes and then told him to go and wash in the pool of Siloam. How foolish he must have looked, groping his way to the pool of Siloam with clay on his eyes. But he was healed.

There was a situation in my own life years ago when I was preaching in East Africa. I held a seven-day series of services and at the end of each message I said, "If anyone wants me to pray for their healing, stand up and I'll pray for you." There was a blind woman led to the meeting by a boy and every day for six days she stood up, I prayed, and nothing happened. I became embarrassed for her. The seventh day she was there again. I said, "If you want me to pray for your healing, stand up!" I closed my eyes and prayed but I could not help wondering, "What's going to happen to that poor woman?" When I opened my eyes, there she was, walking forward without the boy to show that her eyes had been healed! You see, she had to be willing to become a fool first.

Be Careful How and What You Hear

A sixth way to complete the sentence, "If you want God's best" is *be careful how and what you hear.*

Obviously, this relates closely to the previous theme, hear and obey God's voice. We are going on with this theme of hearing.

I have already pointed out that all through the Bible, from the Old Testament into the New, the basic requirement for belonging to God's people is *hearing and obeying His voice.* In the Old Testament, God said to Israel, "Obey My voice, and I will be your God, and you shall be

My people." In the New Testament Jesus said, "My sheep hear my voice, and I know them, and they follow me." That requirement never changes in any dispensation or any age.

We will now consider more of what is involved in hearing God's voice. Jesus said two things at different times in the gospels. He said, "take heed *what* you hear," and later on He said, "take heed *how* you hear." Let us examine both of these statements and see what they have to say to us.

The first one, "...what you hear," is in Mark 4:23–25, where Jesus begins, "If anyone has ears to hear, let him hear." I understand that to mean, "If anyone has ears to hear God's voice, let him hear." I pointed out that we are not born naturally with the ability to hear God's voice. It is something that must be imparted to us by the Holy Spirit. It is something that must be cultivated.

Then Jesus went on to say:

"Take heed what you hear. With the same measure you use, it will be measured to you; and to you who hear, more will be given. For whoever has, to him more will be given; but whoever

*does not have, even what he has will be taken
away from him."*

There are three principles which Jesus
unfolds there. First, the basic requirement is
having the ability to hear; that is, to hear God's
voice. "If anyone has ears to hear, let him hear."

Second, by right hearing (or by listening
to the right thing) we increase our spiritual
resources. "To you who hear," Jesus says, "more
will be given." The same measure that you use
will be measured back to you. The more you give
of yourself to hearing God's voice, the more God
will give Himself back to you. In other words,
we settle the measure with which God will give
Himself to us. The measure with which we hear
is the measure with which God will impart
Himself to us.

The third principle is that by wrong hearing
(or failure to hear) we decrease our spiritual
resources and finally become spiritually bankrupt. Jesus says, " …whoever has, to him more
will be given; but whoever does not have, even
what he has will be taken away from him." In my
experience, I have encountered Christians who

seem to be totally bankrupt, yet in past years they were abounding in the blessing of the Lord. What had bankrupted them? They had lost the ability to hear (had ceased to cultivate that ability) and had begun to listen to the wrong things. They had cut God off and opened themselves up to evil, negative sources, which had bankrupted them spiritually.

Jesus also said, "Be careful *how* you hear."

> *"Therefore take heed how you hear. For whoever has, to him more will be given; and whoever does not have, even what he seems to have will be taken from him."*　　Luke 8:18

Again, the same solemn warning. The way in which we open up to hear God will determine the way in which God imparts Himself to us. But, if we shut God out by wrong hearing, then we become bankrupt. It is the same principle of increase or decrease according to what we hear and how we hear.

I want to mention another word about how to hear; that is, we must learn what to accept and what to reject. There is a very pertinent statement in Job 12:11: "Does not the ear test words as the tongue tastes food?"

The ear fulfills the same function to words that the mouth does to what we eat. We all know that if we take something into our mouth and it is bitter or unpleasant, we do not swallow it, we spit it out. What that statement in Job is saying is that our ears need to do the same to what we hear. If we hear something that is bitter, negative or destructive to our faith, then we should not admit it, we should reject it.

Just as the tongue tastes food, the ear tests words. I have often said to people, "When you listen to a preacher (or whoever is talking) do what you do when you eat fish: swallow the flesh and spit out the bones. If you swallow the bones, you are going to be sorry for it." That is my simple application of what Jesus meant when He said, "Be careful how you hear." Let the right thing in but keep the wrong thing out. If you let the wrong thing in, you will regret it.

Another principle that relates to hearing is stated in Romans 10:17: "So then faith comes by hearing, and hearing by the word of God."

That is a tremendously important truth:

"...faith comes...." You don't need to be without faith. I remember a time when I was without faith. I was sick in a hospital for one year on end and doctors could not heal me; I was hopeless. But one day the Holy Spirit quickened that statement to me, *faith comes*. If you don't have faith, you can get it. How do you get it? By hearing. Hearing what? The Word of God. I began to hear God's Word and through it faith came and eventually I was released from the hospital. I was healed, not by medical means, but by the supernatural power of God because I received faith through hearing the Word of God.

The important thing that I want to emphasize is this: not only does faith come by hearing, but unbelief comes by hearing, too. Paul says this in 2 Timothy 2:16–18, where he is advising Timothy how to lead a successful Christian life.

> *Avoid godless chatter, because those who indulge in it will become more and more ungodly. Their teaching will spread like gangrene* [or cancer, the same word means both]. *Among them are Hymenaeus and Philetus, who have wandered away from the truth. They say that the*

resurrection has already taken place, and they destroy the faith of some.

Paul is saying that if you want to keep your faith, you should not listen to godless chatter or the likes of Hymenaeus and Philetus, who were spreading false teaching. If you go on hearing it, it will enter into your heart and mind and will eat away your faith just like a cancer eats away sound flesh. Cultivate instead the practice of right hearing: what you hear and how you hear. Faith comes by hearing the Word of God.

As a logical consequence, choose your friends and associates with care because they will be the people to whom you will listen the most. You will want to listen to people who have something good to say, not something that destroys your faith.

> *Do not be yoked together with unbelievers. For what do righteousness and wickedness have in common? Or what fellowship can light have with darkness?* 2 Corinthians 6:14

> *Have nothing to do with the fruitless deeds of darkness, but rather expose them. For it is*

shameful even to mention what the disobedient do in secret. Ephesians 5:11–12

Do not associate with people whose speech and conduct is evil. It will poison you spiritually. On the positive side, Paul says this to Timothy:

Flee the evil desires of youth, and pursue righteousness, faith, love, and peace, along with those who call on the Lord out of a pure heart.
2 Timothy 2:22

In other words, if you are going to pursue the good things, you must pursue them in the right company, with those who call on the Lord out of a pure heart.

CHAPTER 9

The Eternal Before the Temporal

The seventh way to complete the sentence is: "If you want God's best, *be more concerned with the eternal than with the temporal.*

There is a passage of Scripture in which the eternal and the temporal are compared and set side by side.

For our light affliction, which is but for a moment, is working for us a far more exceeding and eternal weight of glory, while we do not look at the things which are seen, but at the things which are not seen. For the things which are seen are

61

temporary, but the things which are not seen are
eternal.   2 Corinthians 4:17–18

Paul says there are two categories of things: the eternal and the temporary. The temporary things are the things we can see, the things of this world which we contact with our senses. But the eternal things are unseen. They belong to the invisible, eternal world. He brings out a tremendously important principle: our light affliction works for us an eternal weight of glory while we are looking, not at the things which are seen, but at the things which are not seen. Most of us are going to go through affliction, let's face that fact. Sooner or later in life we are going to face trouble, hardship or difficulty which will do for us something of eternal value on one basic condition: while we continue looking at the things which are not seen. But, if we take our eyes off the eternal and begin to look only at the temporary things, at the things of this world which we contact with our natural senses, then our affliction is no longer working for us that eternal glory which it is God's purpose for us to have.

When we come into trouble or affliction it is

very important that we learn to respond the right way. We must not be distracted from the eternal by problems and troubles, but keep our eyes steadfastly fixed on the eternal and unseen.

Paul deliberately expresses a paradox here when he talks about looking at the things which are not seen. How can you look at things which are not seen? The answer is, of course, that we contact the eternal, not by our physical senses, but by faith. We contact the temporary by the senses; we contact the eternal by our faith.

A little farther on in the same epistle, Paul says that as Christians we walk by faith, not by sight. In other words, we are not primarily influenced by the temporary things of this world that we contact with our senses. Instead, we walk by faith. We are directed, governed, controlled and motivated by the things of the unseen world, which are eternal things.

In 2 Corinthians 3:8 Paul gives another extremely important and related revelation, that the eternal is revealed to us in the mirror of God's Word. In the New Testament the Word of God is often compared to a mirror. We are told that this mirror does not show us our natural, physical body or outward appearance, but it shows us the unseen, eternal things – our spiritual nature and the things of the spiritual world.

> *But we all, with unveiled face, beholding as in a mirror the glory of the Lord, are being transformed into the same image from glory to glory, just as by the Spirit of the Lord.*
>
> 2 Corinthians 3:18

Again, the same principle is brought out. It is only while we look in the mirror of God's Word and see the eternal and the glory which God has prepared for us there, that the Holy Spirit works upon us to transform us into the likeness of that glory. If we take our eyes off the eternal, the Holy Spirit can no longer work His transforming work in us. This is because Jesus is Lord both of the eternal and the temporal. He will bless us in both realms, but only if we keep our priorities right. If our priorities are wrong, then we miss the blessing of the Lord and the Spirit of God is not able to work upon us.

Moses is an example of a man who kept his priorities right. He is described in Hebrews 11:24–27:

By faith Moses, when he became of age, refused to be called the son of Pharaoh's daughter, choosing rather to suffer affliction with the people of God than to enjoy the passing pleasures of sin, esteeming the reproach of Christ greater riches than the treasures in Egypt; for he looked to the reward. By faith he forsook Egypt, not fearing the wrath of the king; for he endured as seeing Him who is invisible.

Notice the key phrase, "... he endured as seeing Him who is invisible." That is the eternal God, the eternal realm and the eternal realities. How did he see them? Not with his senses but by faith. Because he contacted the unseen eternal realities by faith, he was not moved away from his calling and he did not lose his sense of values. He did not esteem the riches of Egypt greater than the eternal riches of God. He was willing to forego the riches of Egypt in order to attain to the eternal riches of God. His priorities were right, because by faith he kept his eyes on the unseen eternal realities.

In this connection, I want to give you a very important warning which is particularly important for people in our contemporary culture and civilization: *Do not pursue riches.* Do not make wealth your goal. Paul has something very sad and very solemn to say to Christians who pursue riches:

> *People who want to get rich fall into temptation and a trap and into many foolish and harmful desires that plunge men into ruin and destruction. For the love of money is a root of all kinds of evil. Some people, eager for money, have wandered from the faith and pierced themselves with many griefs. But you, man of God, flee from all this, and pursue righteousness, godliness, faith, love, endurance and gentleness.*

1 Timothy 6:9–11

Do not pursue riches. Pursue the eternal realities, the eternal riches. If you pursue the temporal riches, if you set your eyes on them and make them your goal, you are going to be sorry. You are going to pierce yourself through with many griefs. You are going to fall into a trap and into "many foolish and harmful desires that plunge men into ruin and destruction." Hear those words and, if that is the way your heart is set, turn back today.

There is an alternative, thank God. The alternative is not that we pursue riches but that we seek the kingdom of God and let God add to us that which we need, in abundance, because God is not stingy but generous. Once He sees that our motives are right, He can release His generosity towards us. Jesus says in Matthew 6:31–33:

"Therefore do not worry, saying, 'What shall we eat?' or 'What shall we drink?' or 'What shall we wear?' For after all these things the Gentiles seek. For your heavenly Father knows that you need all these things. But seek first the kingdom of God and His righteousness [the eternal things] *and all these things* [the temporal things] *shall be added to you."*

There is a great difference between pursuing the temporal – or pursuing the eternal and letting God add the temporal to you. You must have your priorities right.

Let God Choose for You

My final bit of advice if you want God's best is: *let God choose for you.*

I have been deeply impressed by a statement made by John the Baptist:

> John answered and said, "A man can receive nothing unless it has been given to him from heaven." John 3:27

John's disciples were reporting to him that the One whom he declared to be the Messiah was getting more disciples than John and they were expecting that somehow John would get upset about this. But he said, in effect, "So what? A man can receive nothing unless it has been given to him from heaven." Many preachers, churches and religious groups often get upset if somebody else gets more church members, more converts or has a larger ministry. But I think we need to cultivate that attitude of John, that a man can receive nothing unless it has been given to him from heaven.

At one time in my ministry I realized I needed to learn that lesson very carefully. As I meditated on that, I said, "Lord, are you sure that's right? I see a lot of people getting things and I don't see any evidence that they were given from heaven."

The Holy Spirit said to me, "There's a difference between grabbing and receiving." That opened my eyes! I saw so many people, Christians included, busy grabbing, out for all they could get. Many times they were ruthless and unethical in their dealings with fellow Christians and with their fellow human beings. They were just out for what they could get. And God said to me, "That's only grabbing. Whatever you get by grabbing, you will not have forever." The only thing you will ultimately keep is what has been given you from heaven. So why go to all that labor and toil to grab and to get something that you will not be allowed to keep? Why not rest, turn your face toward God and say, "God, show me what it's your good pleasure to give me"?

Jesus said to His disciples, "Fear not, little flock, for it is your Father's good pleasure to give you the kingdom." Brothers and sisters, if we have the kingdom, why do we have to grab? We do not get the kingdom because we grab for it, we get the kingdom because it is God's good pleasure to give us the kingdom. We must learn to rest for a little while from grabbing and be willing to see what God wants to give. Many times when we grab and have that grabbing attitude, we are not in a condition to be able to receive what God is freely offering to us.

I spend much of the year in Israel and there is a phrase that we hear so often, "I've got a right to this; it's mine!" That is a natural way to think, but it is not the way to think in the kingdom of God. In the kingdom of God, we say, "God, my Father, what is it your good pleasure to give me?" That is the only thing that matters. That is the only thing that is permanent.

God said to His people, Israel, in Psalm 47:

For the Lord Most High is to be feared,
A great King over all the earth.
He subdues peoples under us,
and nations under our feet.
He chooses our inheritance for us,
The glory of Jacob whom He loves.

Psalm 47:2–4

God did not tell Israel to go out and look for the best piece of land and grab it. He said He would give them a place that He had chosen. In connection with that land He uses the word *glory*. The Bible says elsewhere that it is the glory of all lands, the beautiful land, the desirable land. God chose much better for them than they would ever have chosen for themselves. When it was a question of them getting their inheritance, He fought for them and He subdued nations under their feet.

If we go out and grab, we do not have God fighting for us. And if we go out and grab, we will probably get in a war that we are going to lose. God will do everything that is needed to bring us into our inheritance.

Another vital point out of the Bible is that our inheritance is the only place we can know true rest. In Deuteronomy 12:9 Moses said to Israel, when they were still east of the Jordan:

"...for as yet you have not come to the rest and the inheritance which the Lord your God is giving you."

Notice that God was giving them their inheritance and, when they came into their inheritance, then they would come into their rest. Why are there so many restless Christians in the world? Because they have never come into their inheritance. Why have they never come into their inheritance? Because they have never allowed God to give it to them. Why have they never allowed God to give it to them? Because they have thought they had to grab it for themselves.

There are a few more important points to make concerning what God gives us. First, there is a tremendous statement made by Jesus in John 10:29. This is the marginal version in more than one of the modern translations. I have also looked at the original Greek text and believe this is the best authenticated original text. "What My Father has given Me is greater than all…"

That is a breathtaking statement! Ultimately, the most important and irresistible thing in the universe; the one thing that is absolutely sure, settled and cannot be challenged or overthrown is the thing which the Father has given. That is greater than all. It is something that no power of hell or demons or evil rulers can ever undo, overthrow or unsettle.

It was characteristic of Jesus that He never wanted anything except what the Father had given. There was no force that could ever take from Jesus what the Father had given. What is true of Him is true, in like measure, of you and me. What the Father has given to you and me is greater than all. Do not get nervous or uptight. The very fact that you get uptight is evidence you are really not moving into what the Father has given you. If you know the Father has given it to you, you can smile at the opposition. It is absolutely guaranteed. The supreme factor in the course of the universe is what God the Father has given.

These are the words of Jesus from the Sermon on the Mount in Matthew 5:5:

"Blessed are the meek, for they shall inherit the earth."

Can you understand that? They do not have to grab the earth, they are going to inherit it. The grabbers will be done away with. There will be an end to all the grabbers – the greedy, the unscrupulous, the covetous, the violent and the wicked. The Bible says they shall be no more. You will search for the wicked man and you will not even find his place. But the meek shall inherit the earth. It is so important that we learn to let God choose our inheritance for us and we apprehend that what the Father has given is greater than all.

Let me close this book on "If You Want God's Best…" by a quotation that I once heard: "God gives His best to those who leave the choice to Him." Are you willing to leave the choice to your Father?

If you want God's best...

...want God's best. Don't settle for less.

...focus on Jesus.

...meditate in God's Word.

...make friends with the Holy Spirit.

...hear and obey God's voice promptly.

...be careful how and what you hear.

...be more concerned with the eternal than the temporal or the temporary. Make sure your priorities are right.

...let God choose for you.

ABOUT THE AUTHOR

Derek Prince (1915–2003) was born in India of British parents. He was educated as a scholar of Greek and Latin at Eton College and King's College, Cambridge in England. Upon graduation he held a fellowship (equivalent to a professorship) in Ancient and Modern Philosophy at King's College. Prince also studied Hebrew, Aramaic, and modern languages at Cambridge and the Hebrew University in Jerusalem. As a student, he was a philosopher and self-proclaimed agnostic.

Bible Teacher

While in the British Medical Corps during World War II, Prince began to study the Bible as a philosophical work. Converted through a powerful encounter with Jesus Christ, he was baptized in the Holy Spirit a few days later. Out of this encounter, he formed two conclusions: first, that Jesus Christ is alive; second, that the Bible is a true, relevant, up-to-date book. These conclusions altered the whole course of his life, which he then devoted to studying and teaching the Bible as the Word of God.

Discharged from the army in Jerusalem in 1945, he married Lydia Christensen, founder of a children's home there. Upon their marriage, he immediately became father to Lydia's eight adopted daughters – six Jewish, one Palestinian Arab, and one English. Together, the family saw the rebirth of the state of Israel in 1948. In the late 1950s, they adopted another daughter while Prince was serving as principal of a teacher training college in Kenya.

In 1963, the Princes immigrated to the United States and pastored a church in Seattle. In 1973, Prince became one of the founders of Intercessors for America. His book *Shaping History through Prayer and Fasting* has awakened Christians around the world to their responsibility to pray for their governments. Many consider underground translations of the book as instrumental in the fall of communist regimes in the USSR, East Germany, and Czechoslovakia.

Lydia Prince died in 1975, and Prince married Ruth Baker (a single mother to three adopted children) in 1978. He met his second wife, like his first wife, while she was serving the Lord in Jerusalem. Ruth died in December 1998 in Jerusalem, where they had lived since 1981.

Teaching, Preaching and Broadcasting

Until a few years before his own death in 2003 at the age of eighty-eight, Prince persisted in the ministry God had called him to as he traveled the world, imparting God's revealed truth, praying for the sick and afflicted, and sharing his prophetic insights into world events in the light of Scripture. Internationally recognized as a Bible scholar and spiritual patriarch, Derek Prince established a teaching ministry that spanned six continents and more than sixty years.

He is the author of more than fifty books, six hundred audio teachings, and one hundred video teachings, many of which have been translated and published in more than one hundred languages.

He pioneered teaching on such groundbreaking themes as generational curses, the biblical significance of Israel, and demonology. Prince's radio program, which began in 1979, has been translated into more than a dozen languages and continues to touch lives. Derek's main gift of explaining the Bible and its teaching in a clear and simple way has helped build a foundation of faith in millions of lives. His nondenominational, nonsectarian approach has made his teaching equally relevant and helpful to people from all racial and religious backgrounds, and his teaching is estimated to have reached more than half the globe.

DPM Worldwide Ministry

In 2002, he said, "It is my desire – and I believe the Lord's desire – that this ministry continue the work, which God began through me over sixty years ago, until Jesus returns." Derek Prince Ministries International continues to reach out to believers in over 140 countries with Derek's teaching, fulfilling the mandate to keep on "until Jesus returns." This is accomplished through the outreaches of more than thirty Derek Prince offices around the world, including primary work in Australia, Canada, China, France, Germany, the Netherlands, New Zealand, Norway, Russia, South Africa, Switzerland, the United Kingdom, and the United States. For current information about these and other worldwide locations, visit www.derekprince.com.

THE GIFTS OF THE SPIRIT

Every believer has been given at least one super-natural gift of the Holy Spirit. Do you know which one you have and how to operate in it?

Prince reveals how to:

- Minister to others through the gifts
- Discern the counterfeit
- Witness through spiritual gifts
- Stir up the gift within you

£9.99
ISBN 978-1-782633-63-1
Paperback and eBook

DEREK PRINCE MINISTRIES
OFFICES WORLDWIDE

DPM – Asia/Pacific
38 Hawdon Street
Sydenham
Christchurch 8023
New Zealand: + 64 3 366 4443
E: admin@dpm.co.nz
W: www.dpm.co.nz and www.derekprince.in

DPM – Australia
15 Park Road
Seven Hills
New South Wales 2147
Australia
T: +61 2 9838 7778
E: enquiries@au.derekprince.com
W: www.derekprince.com.au

DPM – Canada
P.O. Box 8354 Halifax
Nova Scotia B3K 5M1
Canada
T: + 1 902 443 9577
E: enquiries.dpm@eastlink.ca
W: www.derekprince.org

DPM – France
B.P. 31, Route d'Oupia
34210 Olonzac
France
T: + 33 468 913872
E: info@derekprince.fr
W: www.derekprince.fr

DPM – Germany
Söldenhofstr. 10
83308 Trostberg
Germany
T: + 49 8621 64146
E: ibl@ibl-dpm.net
W: www.ibl-dpm.net

DPM – Netherlands
Nijverheidsweg 12
7005 BJ Doetinchem
Netherlands
T: +31 251–255044
E: info@derekprince.nl
W: www.derekprince.nl

DPM – Norway
P.O. Box 129
Lodderfjord
N-5881 Bergen
Norway
T: +47 928 39855
E: sverre@derekprince.no
W: www.derekprince.no

Derek Prince Publications Pte. Ltd.
P.O. Box 2046
Robinson Road Post Office
Singapore 904046
T: + 65 6392 1812
E: dpmchina@singnet.com.sg
W: www.dpmchina.org (English)
    www.ygmweb.org (Chinese)

DPM – South Africa
P.O. Box 33367
Glenstantia
0010 Pretoria
South Africa
T: +27 12 348 9537
E: enquiries@derekprince.co.za
W: www.derekprince.co.za

DPM – Switzerland
Alpenblick 8
CH-8934 Knonau
Switzerland
T: + 41 44 768 25 06
E: dpm-ch@ibl-dpm.net
W: www.ibl-dpm.net

DPM – UK
PO Box 393
Hitchin SG5 9EU
United Kingdom
T: + 44 1462 492100
E: enquiries@dpmuk.org
W: www.dpmuk.org

DPM – USA
P.O. Box 19501
Charlotte NC 28219
USA
T: + 1 704 357 3556
E: ContactUs@derekprince.org
W: www.derekprince.org